THE AVMOR COLLECTION

THE
AVMOR
COLLECTION

Affectionate portraits
of an historic building,
its setting and its place
in the heart
of Old Montreal

May 12/98
To Sue Seley
Lots of good
wishes

Ari and Dora
Moroni

1998

Editor:	Dora Morrow
Editorial consultant:	William Weintraub
Design and typesetting:	Martin Dufour, RCA
Editorial assistant:	Sarah Haggard
Linguistic revision:	Jill Corner
French translation:	Hélène Joly
Photographs:	Mark Montebello
Archive photographs:	McCord Museum of Canadian History, Notman Photographic Archives
Colour separations and films:	Litho Montérégie
Printing and binding:	Métro Litho

ISBN 0-9682946-0-X

Legal deposits:/Dépôt légal
Bibliothèque nationale du Québec, 1998
National Library of Canada, 1998

THE AVMOR COLLECTION
Montreal, (Quebec) Canada

PRINTED AND BOUND IN CANADA.
IMPRIMÉ ET RELIÉ AU CANADA

This book is dedicated to
the people of Avmor,
both past and present employees.

Their spirit, committed efforts
and loyalty have provided
the key to our success.

Ce livre est dédié
aux gens d'Avmor, à ses employés
d'hier et aujourd'hui.

Leur énergie, leur engagement
et leur loyauté demeure
la cle de notre succès.

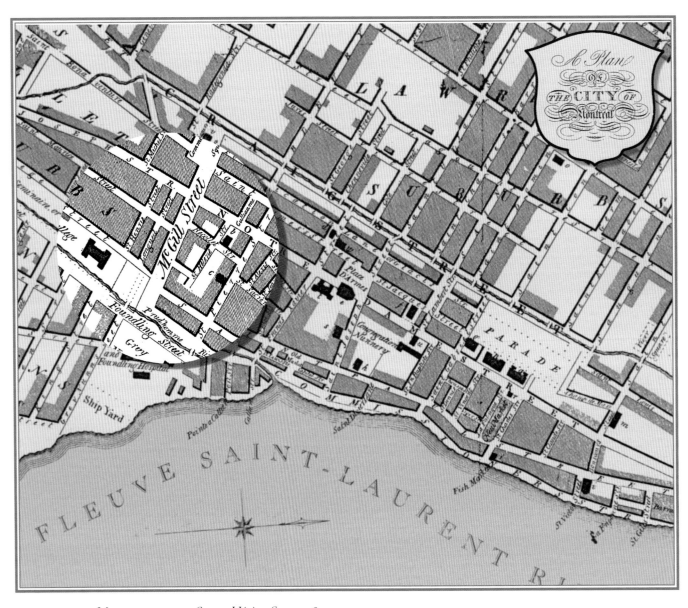

Montreal, showing Sainte-Hélène Street, 1823

CONTENTS

VIEW OF MONTREAL HARBOUR, 1884

HERITAGE MONTREAL

THERE are many important buildings in Old Montreal, buildings of great architectural or historical significance from the seventeenth through the twentieth centuries. However the character of the district is due as much to the streetscapes that define it as to the individual buildings that embellish it.

Sainte-Hélène Street is a remarkable ensemble of nineteenth-century commercial architecture. The composition of buildings and street, the proportions of the greystone facades with their generous window openings and Italianate detailing, are truly exceptional in that they successfully blend the aesthetics of a bygone age with the functional needs of modern business.

These paintings and photographs are a tribute to those who work and live in Old Montreal as well as an intriguing collection of perceptions of the street. We hope that they enable both Montrealers and visitors to perceive the beauty of Sainte-Hélène Street.

OUTRE les édifices et monuments d'une grande valeur architecturale et d'histoire hérités des générations qui se sont succédées du XVIIᵉ au XXᵉ siècle, le Vieux-Montréal tire son caractère de ses rues et des passages bâtis qu'elles présentent. Tant les bijoux d'architecture que le tissu urbain témoignent de l'importance et de la richesse du premier quartier de Montréal.

La rue Sainte-Hélène constitue l'un des ensembles les plus remarquables de ce paysage architectural. Les impressionnantes façades en pierre grise des bâtiments qui l'encadrent, la richesse des détails sculptés et des corniches italianisantes et les généreuses proportions des ouvertures expriment éloquemment les aspirations de l'architecture commerciale du XIXᵉ siècle, combinant fonctionnalité et recherche esthétique.

Outre l'hommage qu'elles rendent à l'engagement de ceux et celles qui travaillent et vivent dans le Vieux-Montréal, les peintures et photographies de la rue Sainte-Hélène figurant dans cet ouvrage présentent une gamme de perceptions de cette rue. Nous espérons qu'elles amèneront Montréalais et visiteurs à faire l'expérience de ce trésor exceptionnel que constitue la rue Sainte-Hélène.

Jacques Cartier Square, 1890

PREFACE

by ALAN STEWART*

IN the historic quarter that is Old Montreal, Sainte-Hélène Street provides a unique window on the history of Montreal. Few other sites in the city can claim a continuous history of occupation since the arrival of the first French settlers in the 1640s, and none so convincingly exemplify the stages of Montreal's development from missionary outpost to commercial metropolis for Canada.

Although located in the extreme western portion of Old Montreal, the neighbourhood of Sainte-Hélène Street originally comprised part of the first farm ever granted on the Island of Montreal. This land was deeded by Paul de Chomedey de Maisonneuve to Pierre Gadois in January 1648, and would remain in the Gadois family for more than forty years. In 1692, Louis XIV permitted the Recollet religious order to establish a monastery at Montreal. Through a series of purchases that year, the Recollets assembled a block of land that had formed part of the Gadois holding and lay within the protective embrace of the town's newly erected palisade. Once this religious community had built its monastery, chapel and various outbuildings, and established its garden and orchards (today the site of Avmor's parking lot), the property underwent few alterations during the remaining decades of the French regime.

With the arrival of the British army in 1760, the function of the Recollet property began to change. Suspicious of the Recollets, the British aimed to suppress the community by attrition; it could continue using its property, but was prohibited from recruiting new members. As early as the 1760s, Anglican and Presbyterian congregations shared the chapel. By the 1790s much of the monastery residence had been converted to military barracks; and during the War of 1812 some twelve hundred soldiers were quartered there. With the death of the last Recollet priest in 1817, title to the property reverted to the British Crown. By the 1850s, Saint-Paul and de la Commune Streets had long been associated with wholesale activities, largely because of their direct access to the port. However as a grow-

---

*ALAN STEWART is Coordinator of the Montreal Research Group, Canadian Centre for Architecture.

ing national market promised greater economic opportunities, companies sought out other locations where goods and supplies could be easily moved. Situated a block away from what was then one of the city's broadest thoroughfares – McGill Street – and having the largest width of any of the old town's north-south streets, Saint-Hélène Street met that requirement. In place of the residences and churches that had lined the street, four and five-storey warehouses were erected between 1854 and 1871. Designed in architectural styles that epitomized the confidence and prosperity of Montreal's business world in the later nineteenth century, these buildings were the same ones that today give Sainte-Hélène Street its rich, unifying character.

Sainte-Hélène Street became home to some of the country's leading commercial wholesaling establishments: Robert Linton & Company (importers and dealers in British and foreign dry goods); Gault Brothers & Company ("the most active and extensive dry

14

St. Urbain Street, 1859

goods importing house in the Canadian Metropolis" with a sales force of about seventy-five clerks in 1893); James Hutton & Company (cutlery, edgetools, and steel); Cassils, Stinson & Company (leather and leather-working tools); James Johnston & Company (dry goods); John A. Paterson (millinery and fancy dry goods); Brown & Claggett (clothiers who claimed they could outfit clients for half what it would cost in New York City); and W. R. Brock Company (carpets). In their display rooms, these businesses showcased the diversity of quality products that the Industrial Revolution made possible.

Over time the wholesaling function of Sainte-Hélène Street has disappeared. That the buildings themselves have been saved from dilapidation and demolition is owed largely to the efforts of committed individuals and organizations who, since the 1960s, have recognized the importance of retaining and recycling these valuable reminders of Montreal's past.

Bonsecours Market, Commissioners Street, 1908

VISION OF A STREET
by WILLIAM WEINTRAUB*

EHOUDA CHAKI sees the street as a celebration. His painting endows it with flags and festivity, the bright colours of Old Montreal in the tourist season. John Little's canvas gives us a sombre, pensive view of this same street, now in mid-winter, blanketed in snow. Parked at the curb, a solitary car emphasizes the lonely stillness of a Sunday morning. William Martucci's painting interprets the street in yet another way, hot in the sunlight of late afternoon, the buildings somehow suggestive of a town in the Old West. One expects a cowboy or an old prospector to come loping around the corner, not a businessman with a briefcase hurrying toward his office.

This is Sainte-Hélène Street, home of Avmor, a Canadian industry leader whose products are sold around the world. During the past three decades, Avrum Morrow, Avmor's president, has commissioned a number of artists to create paintings, drawings and photographs of Sainte-Hélène Street, and their work is displayed throughout the company's offices. Besides these works by professional artists, several amateurs have contributed to this collection of pictures, which offers striking testimony of how unique is every artist's vision, how infinite the number of ways in which art can view the same subject.

Sainte-Hélène Street, in the western part of Old Montreal, stretches south from Notre Dame Street to Le Moyne Street. Although only two blocks long, it is redolent of the history of Montreal and of the optimism and enterprise that built a great city. In the year 1800, before Sainte-Hélène Street existed, Montreal was still a small fortified town enclosed by thick stone walls eighteen feet high. These had been erected in the previous century by the government of New France to repel Iroquois or British assailants. But now, under the British flag, the walls were deemed to serve no further purpose and constituted a hindrance to the expansion of the town. The long process of tearing them down was completed in 1817 and Sainte-Hélène Street was opened the following year. It was a street destined to flourish amid the industrial and commercial growth of the nineteenth century. Elegant

---

* WILLIAM WEINTRAUB is a Montreal author and filmmaker.

buildings would arise here, reflecting the
Victorian taste for combining elegance with
solidity, some of the structures being
inspired by the Italian Renaissance style,
with occasional Second Empire embellish-
ments.

Among the businesses located on
Sainte-Hélène Street in bygone days were
Forbes Bros., purveyors of foodstuffs to
restaurants and hotels; Chase and Sanborn,
which roasted its coffee in large gas-fired
vats; and Brown and Claggett's Recollet
House department store, offering dry
goods to the carriage trade (including silks
that astonished a *Gazette* reporter of the
time by costing \$7.50 a yard). It is in the
historic greystone buildings that once
housed these enterprises that Avmor now
has its factory and offices, occupying
70,000 square feet of space, plus a 10,000

McGill Street, 1875

square-foot parking lot at the corner of Sainte-Hélene and Le Moyne Streets.

During the 1950s, Montreal's industrial growth was spreading from the centre of the
city to outlying areas of the island, and eventually across to the north and south shores
where land was cheap and transportation rapidly expanding. But Avmor chose to stay in
the area that would eventually come to be known as Old Montreal, an outstanding attrac-
tion for tourists, protected by zoning regulations to preserve its historical character. In this
context, Avmor is proud of its role in helping to maintain the architectural integrity of the
street.

Avrum Morrow has always valued the positive influence of art in our lives. His com-
missioning of the works that can be seen on the pages of this book reflects his lifelong
fascination with visual inventiveness. He hopes that readers will now share the delight that
employees and visitors have long taken in Avmor's premises – affectionate and insightful
portraits of a remarkable subject.

THE PLEASURES OF THIS PROJECT
by Avrum Morrow

Ommissioning paintings and photographs for Avmor's offices has given me enormous pleasure. Now, in having them reproduced in this book, I hope to share this pleasure with others. Also, I would hope to share, in some measure, what for me was another of the project's benefits – the expansion of my understanding of the artistic process. I have long recognized the dimension that art brings to our lives, how it is a force that can make life more thoughtful, creative and open. The project of assembling this collection of art has given me many new insights into the mysteries of creativity and I have been particularly fascinated to see what a great variety of differing visions can be inspired by the same landscape – or perhaps I should say cityscape.

In discussions with a number of the artists involved, I came to understand the highly individual concepts that lay behind the work they executed. For instance, Gentile Tondino, whose painting is seen on page 63, explained why he did not show the boundary of the Avmor property, letting the image extend on both sides of the frame. He felt that this would suggest the repetitions in form and decoration which give unity to other parts of Old Montreal. Seeing this, I realized how a picture can somehow evoke images well beyond its own boundaries.

Over the years, I derived much pleasure from searching out talented artists and persuading them to accept a rather peculiar assignment – a work of art for our offices. I had long admired the work of Gavin Affleck, a leading architect who is also a serious painter, but I wondered whether he would be willing to paint a picture for us. When I put my question to him, he thought it over for a moment and then agreed, telling me, with disarming frankness, that he would like the challenge of doing something he would not normally undertake, And I was very happy when he delivered the painting shown on page 23.

Brian Kipping (pages 40-41) is an artist who had to be lured back to Montreal. I first saw his work at a gallery in Toronto, where he lives and works, and I immediately decided that our walls had to have a contribution from him. It wasn't too difficult to get him to come to Montreal and put up his easel on Sainte-Hélène Street. He had worked in Montreal before and knew that a visit would give him the opportunity of feasting on our unparalleled bagels and smoked meat.

In finding artists, I had help from a valued scout – Mattie Chinks, Avmor's president. Mattie first saw the work of Andris Leimanis in the garden of the Ritz Carlton Hotel in a summertime display. Mattie introduced Andris to me and the happy result is the painting to be seen on page 45.

For two of the artists, I did not have to go very far afield, as they are members of my family. One of the most versatile of the painters I commissioned is my niece, Nina Berkson, who earns her living as a much sought-after illustrator who also loves to paint. The picture she did for Avmor (page 25) confirmed my assessment of her formidable talent. Morris Fish, who is married to another of my nieces, is a judge of the Quebec Court of Appeal as well as being an enthusiastic amateur painter. The family is especially proud of his contribution to Avmor's collection.

In one case I was able to watch two of the artists at work, although not on the paintings they contributed to our collection. It was a strange and unforgettable experience to spend an afternoon watching Seymour Segal (pages 58-59) and Yehouda Chaki (pages 28-29) painting swiftly and in tandem on a huge mural at the Saidye Bronfman Centre. After their spectacular work was completed, they cut it up, the pieces to be sold to raise scholarship money for aspiring young artists.

Some of the artists have become good friends of mine. Chaki and I occasionally enjoy a pleasantly disputatious chat over a glass of arak, that potent Middle Eastern intoxicant. And with John Little (pages 46-49) I enjoy conversations about hockey, always amazed at his passion for the game and his encyclopedic knowledge of it. Which other Canadian artist can reel off the names of all the players of the Montreal Maroons of 1935?

My contact with all these painters and photographers emboldened me one day to try my own hand at artistic creation. What resulted was not a painting and not a photograph, but I like to think that it intrigues people who notice it in the lobby of the Avmor building. If you're curious, you can learn about it on page 69.

THE
AVMOR
COLLECTION

GAVIN AFFLECK

AVIN AFFLECK was born in Montreal in 1958. He studied art at CEGEP du Vieux Montréal (1978); at the Saidye Bronfman Centre School of Fine Arts with Ghitta Caiserman-Roth, Yehouda Chaki and Moe Reinblatt (1979-1981); at Concordia University School of Fine Arts with John Miller, Yves Gaucher and Guido Molinari (1980-1983); and at the McGill University School of Architecture (1980-1985).

In addition to being a member of the Order of Architects of Quebec since 1988 and sitting on numerous professional juries and committees, Affleck teaches part-time at the McGill University School of Architecture, and serves as a guest critic at the schools of architecture at Laval University, the Université de Montréal, the Université du Québec à Montréal and the University of Manitoba.

He has participated in numerous group exhibitions throughout Quebec, as well as in several solo exhibitions in Montreal, notably at the Galerie Les Deux B, the Timothy Roberts Gallery, the McGill University Faculty Club and the Galerie Max Gauvin. His work is also represented in private collections in France, the U. S. and across Canada.

The Avmor collection provides young artists like Gavin Affleck with another opportunity to explore their interest in the unique architectural character of Old Montreal.

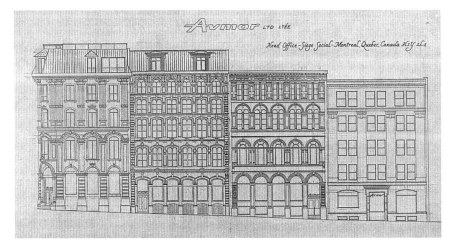

Architectural drawing, 1994
25″ x 54½″ (63.5 x 138.4 cm)

Oil on canvas, 1994
40″ x 30″ (101.6 x 76.2 cm)

NINA BERKSON

NINA BERKSON began studying fine art in
Montreal at Dawson College, and film
animation at the now defunct Montreal
Museum of Fine Arts School. In the early eighties
she pursued her interest in illustration and design
at Toronto's Sheridan College of Applied Arts &
Technology, and at the Ontario College of Art.

She has worked as a freelance illustrator since
1979, winning numerous awards and honours in a
distinguished career. She earned a gold award in
1995, silver awards in 1993 and 1994, and awards of
merit in 1993 and 1995 at the annual CAPIC
National Show. She was granted awards of excel-
lence from the prestigious American magazine
Communication Arts and from Centre Design
UQAM, and received a bronze award for her Dairy
Bureau of Canada's *Butter* commercial at the New
York Film Festival in 1990.

Berkson's clients have included Canada Post,
the Dairy Bureau of Canada, 3M, VISA, Air
Canada, the Royal Bank of Canada, American
Express, Weight Watchers, Eaton's, Holt Renfrew,
Hydro-Québec, Birks, Labatt Breweries, American
Airlines, *Vanity Fair*, *Playboy*, the Toronto Humane
Society and the *Globe and Mail*.

Oil on canvas, 1989
36″ x 36″ (94 x 94 cm)

GHITTA CAISERMAN-ROTH, RCA

GHITTA CAISERMAN-ROTH was born in Montreal and grew up on Esplanade Avenue in the heart of the city. She still lives in the area with her architect husband Max Roth. A graduate of the Parsons School of Design in New York with a post-graduate scholarship, she also studied at the American Artists' School with Harry Sternberg at the Art Students' League and with the painter Moses Soyer.

Throughout her life she has maintained a very active profile as artist, teacher and lecturer. She is a member of the Royal Canadian Academy, the Conseil des artistes peintres du Québec and the Conseil québécois de l'estampe. She is also president of Atelier Graphia 3710, and currently serves as vice-chair of the Government of Canada's Commission on the Status of the Artist.

Her numerous honours include the Canadian Centennial Medal and a Canada Council Senior Fellowship. She taught for many years at Sir George Williams College and Concordia University, at the Saidye Bronfman Centre, and at summer schools at Queen's University, Mount Allison University, the Nova Scotia College of Art, Mount St. Vincent University, John Abbott College, and other institutions. She has lectured extensively in Canada and the U.S., has served as an art critic for the CBC, and continues to give critiques to individual artists and education groups.

Solo exhibitions include the Galerie Quartier des Arts in Pointe Claire, Galerie 007 in Bochum, Germany, the Galerie de l'Art Français in Montreal, the École des Hautes études commerciales, the Université de Montréal, the Ariel Gallery of Tula, Atlanta and the Robertson Gallery in Ottawa, among others.

Public and corporate collectors of her work include Air Canada, the Canadian Government Art Bank, the Art Gallery of Ontario, the Beaverbrook Art Gallery, the Department of External Affairs, the Kitchener-Waterloo Art Gallery, the McMichael Conservation Gallery at Kleinberg, the Montreal Museum of Fine Arts, the National Gallery of Canada, Bank Leumi, Israel, the Musée du Québec, Provigo, Pratt & Whitney, Steinberg, the Banque Nationale de Paris, MacLean-Hunter, New York Life and VIA Rail.

Her subject matter is derived from a personal view of her life experience – imagery of people, feelings, social concerns, landscape, interiors that often move from nature into symbol, and always an attempt to integrate medium, art language and theme.

"I approached the painting for Avmor by separating some of the elements involved – architectural shapes, reflections, sunlight and shadow – then tried to interact them through transparency, tried to capture the reality of the place and at the same time trying to personalize the painting."

Oil on canvas, 1994
30″ x 40″ (76.2 x 101.6 cm)

27

YEHOUDA CHAKI

YEHOUDA CHAKI was born in Athens, Greece in 1938. He lived in Tel Aviv from 1945 to 1960, in Paris from 1960 until 1963, and has since lived in Montreal. He studied art in Tel Aviv under Professor Joseph Schwartzman and at the Avni Academi of Art, and in Paris at the École des Beaux-Arts. From 1967 to 1989 he served as head of painting and drawing in the Department of Fine Arts at the Saidye Bronfman Centre; since then he has worked as an artistic advisor to the Centre.

Over a thirty-year period Chaki has enjoyed many solo exhibitions throughout Canada, the United States and Israel, and has participated in a number of group exhibitions in Canada, the U.S., France and Brazil. In recent years his work has been shown at the international art fairs in New York, Miami, Los Angeles and Tokyo.

Chaki's work is found in nearly fifty public collections around the world, including the Canadian Embassy in Argentina and the Canadian Consulate in New York, the Rose Museum in Boston, the Philadelphia Museum, the Beaverbrook Art Gallery, the Montreal Museum of Fine Arts, the Musée d'art contemporain de Montréal, the Musée d'art juif in Paris, Ben-Gurion University, and the Fort Lauderdale Museum, as well as in the corporate collections of companies such as SNC-Lavalin, the Royal Bank of Canada, Imperial Oil, Coca-Cola and General Electric.

Chaki's vibrant and expressionist painting of the Avmor building situates it in the heart of Old Montreal, in the dynamic social and political context of this fascinating multicultural city.

Gouache on paper, 1992
22″ X 30″ (55.9 X 76.2 cm)

28

29

JOHN COLLINS

John Collins was born in Washington, D.C. in 1917, and came to Montreal as a child. He studied art at both the École des Beaux Arts and Sir George Williams College Art School.

At the Montreal *Gazette*, where he published innumerable cartoons and illustrations before retiring in 1982, his working career spanned a remarkable forty-four years. He won two National Newspaper Awards for editorial cartooning and was a member and one-time President of the Association of American Editorial Cartoonists.

As a watercolourist he exhibited in the Spring Shows of the Montreal Museum of Fine Arts and at the Royal Academy of Arts. He was awarded the Jessie Dow Prize for Watercolours in a Montreal Museum of Fine Arts exhibition.

He has participated in a three-man show at the Montreal Museum of Fine Arts, an exhibition at the Arts Club, and also in numerous group shows at the Lakeshore Association of Artists, of which he is a former president. Over the years he has had several solo exhibitions at Dan Delaney's Artlenders Galleries, and as an illustrator has produced many of the sketches published in Edgar Andrew Collard's historical column "All Our Yesterdays" in the Montreal *Gazette*.

Pen sketch, 1988
22″ x 28½″ (55.9 x 72.4 cm)

Rue Sainte-Hélène

31

JOAN EDWARD

JOAN EDWARD was born and raised in Montreal and spent several years studying and working in Vancouver, Ottawa and London, England. She currently lives in Newfoundland.

She has pursued music and art throughout her life. She studied piano with George M. Brewer and received her Performer's Licentiate in 1942, the same year she graduated from McGill University with a Bachelor of Arts degree. In 1943 she entered the education faculty at McGill, and then taught at public schools in Montreal and in North Vancouver.

Her art studies included evening classes in oil painting at the Vancouver School of Art; a summer spent at the Banff School of Fine Arts (1945) where she received the Brewster Scholarship; night classes with André Masson while in Ottawa with the NFB; and later, classes in life drawing at the Montreal Museum of Fine Arts with Moe Reinblatt. After studying music in London, she returned to Canada and spent eleven years at the National Film Board as a film music editor. Since that time she has taught piano privately while concurrently pursuing her painting.

Joan Edward has had many solo exhibitions of portraits and landscapes, notably at the Westmount Public Library, the Fraser-Hickson Institute, the Reginald Dawson Library and McGill University Faculty Club. She has also participated in juried group shows, including Arts Club shows at the Klinkoff Gallery, Ogilvy's Tudor Hall and the Arts Club; at the Rose Window Gallery in Knowlton; at the 50 Painters of Quebec show in Farnham; and at the Laval Community Centre. She has also exhibited in Vermont.

Edward's works are found in both private and corporate collections, and Avmor is proud to include her sensitive pen sketch in its collection.

Ink drawing on paper, 1995
13″ x 10¼″ (33 x 26 cm)

LISA S. ELIN

Lisa Elin's training as a building technician and architectural draughtsman has led her into an unusual occupation – the creation of small plaster models of interesting houses, institutions and commercial buildings. These delightful miniature replicas are executed with painstaking attention to detail, and her depiction of the Avmor Building took more than one hundred hours to sculpt.

Among Elin's other significant commissions are the Westmount Public Library and the Maison Alcan buildings on Sherbrooke Street in Montreal. But most of her work involves private residences; models commissioned by people who want a memento of their house. She has been doing this kind of work since 1992, through the company she created – Architexture Montreal.

After studying the facade of a building, she photographs it and then makes a mould by carving it in wax. After casting the model in plaster, she carefully paints it, endeavouring to match the original as closely as possible. Where relevant, she adds bushes and flowers.

Architecture has long been a passion for this artist, who was born in 1968. At the age of twelve, she was already designing houses and floor plans. Her studies at Dawson College and Montreal Technical College culminated in an A.E.C. in architectural draughting and building technology. Besides her business in creating miniature buildings, she is working on organizing, restoring and recording the City of Westmount's extensive architectural archives.

Painted plaster, 1997
6½″ x 10½″ (16.5 x 26.7 cm)

MORRIS FISH

For more than three decades Morris Fish has enjoyed a close relationship with the Avmor family. He was born in Montreal, where he received his primary and secondary education. While a law student he was editor-in-chief of the *McGill Daily* and worked as a staff reporter for the *Montreal Star*.

He later did post-graduate work at the Faculté de droit et des sciences économiques, Université de Paris, while reporting for the *Montreal Star* and for other Canadian newspapers from Sweden, the Soviet Union, France, the Middle East and Japan. He has for many years been interested in photography, ceramics, sculpture and painting. Several of his photographs have appeared in books and magazines.

After twenty-five years as a defence counsel and member of the Bars of Quebec, Alberta and Prince Edward Island, he was appointed to the Quebec Court of Appeal in 1989. He has lectured in criminal law at the University of Ottawa, the Université de Montréal and McGill University, where he chairs the Law Faculty's Advisory Council.

When time permits, he still makes pictures.

Colour photograph, 1989
13¾″ x 10½″ (34.9 x 26.7 cm)

NORMAND HUDON

ORN in Montreal in 1929, Normand Hudon studied at the École des Beaux-Arts with Jean Simard and René Chicoine, and in Paris at the Académie de Montmartre with Fernand Léger. His debut was at the First Exhibition of Caricaturists of Canada in 1948, the same year he bagan working as a cartoonist for *La Patrie* and *Le Petit Journal*.

During a long and varied career Hudon contributed cartoons to *La Presse, Allo-Police, Cité Libre, Le Clairon, Le Journal de Montréal, Le Poing* and *Le Quartier Latin*. He produced posters for the Montreal World Film Festival, les Grands Ballets Canadiens, the Montreal Museum of Fine Arts, the Théâtre du Nouveau-Monde, the Théâtre du Rideau-Verte and Vins de France. His output includes a number of books, murals, and record and book jackets. In 1965 he was commissioned to design a cover for *Time* magazine; a satirical portrait of Guy Favreau. In 1967 he received critical attention for his work commissioned by Canada at Expo '67.

Hudon's first major solo show was held at the Galerie Agnès-Lefort and followed by an exhibition of 350 cartoons at the Restaurant Hélène de Champlain. Other solo shows included the Waddington Gallery, Place des Arts, the Galerie Alexandre, the Galerie Clarence-Gagnon, the Galerie Gilles-Brown, the Musée de Vaudreuil, the Maison d'art Saint-Laurent, Le Balcon d'art and the Galerie Beauchamp-Joncas. His work is represented in many public and private collections.

In 1966 Hudon created a satirical history of Avmor's sanitation products in a new art form that he called "stop art." His collage technique comprised a number of rectangular units, each a complete composition but all blended into one image. He called it "stop art" because the viewer must stop to appreciate each unit within the whole.

Normand Hudon died in January, 1997.

Collage on board, 1966
30″ x 24″ (76.2 x 61 cm)

BRIAN KIPPING

BRIAN KIPPING was born in 1953 in Edmonton, Alberta, and currently lives and works in Toronto. He studied art at the Ontario College of Art from 1970 to 1974, and served as curator of Gallery 76 in Toronto from 1975 to 1977.

He has participated in numerous solo and group exhibitions in Ottawa, Montreal, Toronto and Vancouver. His work is found in many public collections, including the Robert McLaughlin Gallery, Hart House, the University of Toronto, the Canada Council Art Bank, the Windsor Art Gallery, the Lavalin Collection, Petro-Canada, Imperial Oil, The Toronto-Dominion Bank, the Musée d'art contemporain de Montréal, General Foods and Norcen Energy Resources.

Brian Kipping paints the colours and textures of contemporary Canadian cities, and was commissioned by Avmor in 1992. Although his work is perceived to be about the structures he depicts, his primary concern is to capture the effects of light. The structural details of his subject are worked out through the use of photographs, and then the image is translated into oil. He adds to the Avmor Collection a subtle painting that evokes the mystery of Old Montreal.

Oil on linen, 1992
18″ x 24″ (45.7 x 61 cm)

GUY LEGARÉ

Guy Legaré was born in Quebec City in 1941, where he trained in industrial design at the Institut de technologie de Québec. Always interested in art, from the age of eight he took painting classes at the Institut des Beaux-Arts and was tutored by a number of private art teachers.

Legaré moved to Montreal in the early sixties to work for the CBC and Radio-Canada as a cameraman and studio director. Painting became his parallel career, and since 1980 he has regularly exhibited his work in both solo and group shows, including the Continental Gallery and the Galerie Clarence-Gagnon in Montreal, the Galerie Vincent in Hull, the Galerie d'art à Saint Adèle, the Galerie Les Mécènes in Rouyn-Noranda, Sensation in Sherbrooke, the Galerie Basque in Rimouski, and Art et style in Baie Saint-Paul.

Over the years he has participated in numerous workshops and conferences throughout the province of Quebec. He was a founding member of the groupe Espace-Fleuve, and served as honorary president of the 1993 summer painting symposium of the Eastern Townships in Magog-Orford. In 1996 he was awarded first prize at the Symposium de peinture de Kamouraska.

Legaré's work is found in several private and corporate collections, notably the Royal Bank of Canada, the Canadian Imperial Bank of Commerce, Bell Canada, Hydro-Québec, Heritage Canada, the Musée de Radio-Canada, Dupont Canada, Caisses populaires Desjardins, Tilden Canada and the municipal collections of Saint-Eustache, Baie-Comeau, Rosemère, Mirabel and Shawinigan.

Guy Legaré paints at a time of day when few people venture forth. Rising as early as four in the morning, he works outdoors to capture the warm tones of the earliest light.

Oil on canvas, 1996
12″ x 16″ (30.5 x 40.7 cm)

ANDRIS LEIMANIS

ANDRIS LEIMANIS was born in Riga, Latvia in 1938 and has lived in Montreal since 1965. Although he began his fine art career in the mid-seventies, he has worked in the field of art since his teens. He has had an active career as an illustrator and commercial art director in both Montreal and Toronto.

Leimanis received his formal and art education in Quebec and New York State. He graduated *cum laude* from Loyola College of Montreal with a Bachelor of Arts degree in 1974 and received a Master of Fine Arts degree from Syracuse University in 1976. Since then he has had both solo and group exhibitions, including the Galerie de Bellefeuille, the Galerie J. Lukacs and the Galerie Bernard Desroches in Montreal, the Kaspar Gallery in Toronto and the Mihalis Gallery in Boca Raton, Florida.

His work is found in private and corporate collections throughout Canada and the U.S., notably the Royal Bank of Canada, Bombardier, Imperial Oil, Texaco Canada, Bell Canada, Northern Telecom, Loblaw's, Gordon Securities, Labatt Breweries, Dofasco, Sun Life Assurance Company of Canada and Canadian Airlines.

Leimanis's painting of the Avmor building on Sainte-Hélène Street captures subtle colour tones and nuances of light. When you look at this picture, the snow seems to be actually falling.

Oil on canvas, 1988
30″ x 40″ (76.2 x 101.6 cm)

JOHN LITTLE, RCA

JOHN LITTLE was born in 1928 and grew up in Montreal's Town of Mount Royal. He left high school after the ninth grade to attend art school at the Monument National, then at the Art Association of Montreal with Arther Lismer and Goodridge Roberts. In 1947 he moved to New York City to study at the Art Students' League.

In 1948 he was employed as an assistant to Ray Bailley on his comic strip "The Adventures of Bruce Gentry". The following year he returned to Montreal to work as a draughtsman in his architect father's office while developing his painting skills.

The Watson Gallery was an early supporter of Little's work and continued to exhibit his paintings until Mr. Watson's retirement. Little then moved to the Continental Gallery where he earned a growing reputation. He produced several covers for *Maclean's Magazine*, and 1961 became an associate of the Royal Canadian Academy of Art. He has always enjoyed a strong following.

Little's work is represented at the National Gallery of Canada, the Beaverbrook Art Gallery and The Sir George Williams University collection of art.

John Little is particularly interested in the older areas in New York City, Montreal and elsewhere, and has an extensive photo collection portraying old urban neighbourhoods. He has always been interested in portraying city life – city streets in particular. He first painted Sainte-Hélène Street in the summer of 1981 and the following year depicted it in wintertime.

Oil on canvas, 1981
24″ x 30″ (61 x 76.2 cm)

46

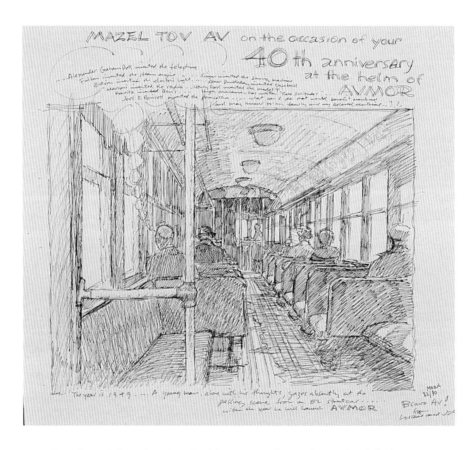

When John Little learned of Avmor's 40th anniversary he sent this unsolicited sketch. He is an longtime friend who loves receiving the annual Avmor apples at Thanksgiving.

Pen sketch, 1990
18" x 20" (45.2 x 52.1 cm)

Oil on canvas, 1982
24" x 30" (61 x 76.2 cm)

WILLIAM MARTUCCI

BORN in 1922, William Martucci showed early promise as an artist but did not decide to become a painter until after returning from the war in 1946, when he enrolled as a student at the Montreal Art Association. His teachers there were Arthur Lismer, Jacques de Tonnancour and Goodridge Roberts. He went on to study with Ghitta Caiserman and Alfred Pinsky at the Montreal Artists' School, where he was introduced to the work of the social realists of that period, notably the Americans Ben Shahn and Jack Levine.

Martucci worked in the U.S. as an assistant to the renowned Italian mural and fresco artist Guido Nincheri. Although he made his living as a professional drummer, he never put down his paintbrush. "There is so much to be said about human deprivation and human warmth... The subject matter of my paintings has changed over the years, the message hasn't. If you look carefully you'll see that. And my idols are still Ben Shahn, Rembrandt and Daumier – they had a feeling for humanity..."

In his later years Martucci found his second wind as a painter, returning to the essentials. Whether still life, cityscape, landscape or portrait, the sparseness and simplicity of his compositions, with their glowing colours, evoke a sense of mystery.

Martucci was equally at home with oil, watercolour, pastel and pen-and-ink. He exhibited at the Art Gallery of Ontario, the Winnipeg Art Gallery and the Montreal Museum of Fine Arts. His work is found in private and corporate collections in Berlin, New York, Toronto, Montreal, Winnipeg and Ottawa.

William Martucci died in 1997.

Watercolour on paper, 1989
8″ x 8½″ (20.3 x 21.6 cm)

Oil on canvas, 1989
20″ x 24″ (50.8 x 61 cm)

SEAN OSBORNE

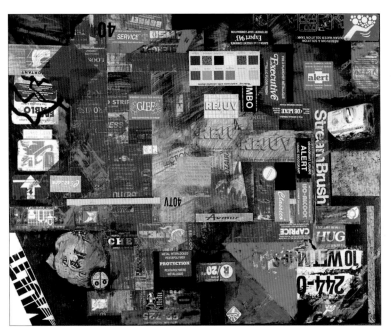

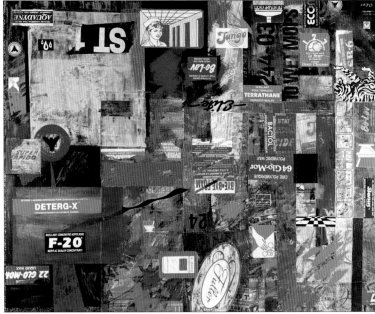

Sean Osborne has a degree in fine arts from Concordia University in Montreal, where he specialized in film production. Despite his commitment to painting, most of his time has been devoted to developing filmmaking skills, including screenplay writing and editing.

He worked for five years as a decorative painter with interior designers such as Montreal's Havie Walker and Toronto's Sandra McGillivray. Projects included retail stores, commercial showrooms and private residences. Some of his clients, in addition to Avmor, included Hallmark of Canada, Empire Electric and the country estate of an international film producer.

He is for the most part a self-taught and self-directed visual artist generally concerned with technology and the human condition. His experience has included producing, directing and editing television commercials with Canadian Thunderlight Films.

With his partner and wife, Jayne Mason, he has executed numerous customized backdrops for television commercials, feature films and television shows, including Ford Motors, Ontario Milk and BC TEL. Their interior decoration and painting business continues to evolve, and they have created elegant surfaces inside many distinguished private residences. Their work ranges from life-like *faux-*

marbre to trompe l'oeil borders and architectural detailing.

In 1993 Osborne produced a mural for the Avmor entrance called *The Avmor Family*. This mural was created using a decoupage technique and comprises four panels laid out end to end. It depicts the wide range of Avmor's products — from barbecue cleaner to washroom specialties — and constitutes a striking portrait of the always environmentally-friendly product line.

Collage on board, 1993
Four panels, each 31″ x 38½″ (78.7 x 97.7 cm)

GERRI PANTEL

BEFORE becoming Avmor's artistic director in 1994, Gerri Pantel was involved in a wide variety of other artistic and educational endeavours. As a freelance designer, she created many concepts for logos, labels and literature, decorated clothing and gifts for women and children and worked in commercial window decor.

Before embarking on her career in design, she worked as an early childhood educator in Montreal schools and as director for arts and crafts programmes in summer camps in Montreal and the Laurentians.

Gerri Pantel has studied art and education at several Montreal institutions, including McGill University, the Université du Québec à Montréal, Dawson College and Sir George Williams University. Her works, in watercolours and acrylics have been exhibited in local group shows.

Acrylic on cotton, 1996
14″ x 18″ (35.6 x 45.7 cm)

PIERRE PIVET

PIERRE PIVET was born in November 1948 in Guilberville, Normandy and grew up in Paris. He was always preoccupied with drawing and painting, and by the age of fifteen had acquired a small art-history library ranging from the classic works of the old masters to those of Cubist era.

On losing both parents at the age of nineteen, Pivet left school to work in the new world of computers at IBM, but continued with night courses at the École des art appliqués in Paris. In 1972 he moved to San Francisco and travelled throughout the western U.S., Mexico and Guatemala before returning to Paris to begin full-time studies at the Académie Port-Royal with Claude Schurr and Jean Marzelle. In 1976 he won the Académie's top prize. Then followed his first solo exhibition at the Galerie Chardin and the start of his career in Europe and North America.

From 1977 to 1983 Pivet travelled extensively in Europe with frequent visits to Morocco. Various trips since then have continued to nurture his interest in the cultures and colours of other countries. Since 1983 he has lived in Montreal.

He has exhibited widely. Venues have included the Alliance française in San Francisco, the Galerie Girafe in Caen, France, the Galerie F.I.A.P., the Galerie Chardin and Galerie Mandragore in Paris, the Galerie Municipale in Limoges, the Galerie Théâtre in Geneva, the Galerie Art Moderne in Luxembourg, the Gallery Noblesse Oblige and the Gallery Daniel in Fort Lauderdale, the Palm Springs Gallery, the Wallace Art Gallery in Calgary, the West End Gallery in Edmonton, the Hollander York Gallery in Toronto, and the Galerie l'Isle in Montreal.

Pierre Pivet's paintings are found in private and public collections throughout Canada, the U.S. and Europe.

Oil on canvas, 1995
36″ x 30″ (91.4 x 76.2 cm)

SEYMOUR SEGAL

SEYMOUR SEGAL is a painter and educator whose work appears in art collections all over the world. Born in Montreal in 1939, he is a self-taught artist and a teacher whose interactive approach has been concerned with helping people engage their internal worlds. He has conducted art workshops for over thirty years, not only for art students at all levels and ages but also for participants from many other sectors, including the medical, financial, service, professional and business fields.

Segal is represented in a number of public collections, notably the Canada Council Art Bank, the Musée du Québec, the Montreal Museum of Fine Arts, the Kitchener-Waterloo Art Gallery, the Université du Québec à Montréal, the Lavalin Collection, the Musée d'art contemporain de Montréal, the Claridge Collection, Cemp Investments, Reitmans, David Hughes Corporation and Graylands Teachers College in Perth, Australia. His paintings are found in private collections throughout Canada, the U.S., Great Britain, Switzerland, Australia, New Zealand and Japan.

When asked why he painted the Avmor buildings so colourfully, he said that every time he visited the Avmor premises he observed a great deal of human activity and "hustle and bustle." He wanted his painting of the facade to reflect this inner vibrancy and to express the energy of the people working inside.

Oil on canvas, 1996
33½″ x 39½″ (85 x 100.3 cm)

58

59

GABOR SZILASI, RCA

Gabor Szilasi was born in Budapest, Hungary in 1928. He emigrated to Canada in 1957 and has lived in Montreal since 1959. Although he has participated in practical and theoretical workshops as well as internships between 1962 and 1976, he is primarily a self-taught photographer.

From 1959 until 1971 Szilasi worked for the Office du film du Québec in Montreal. Since then he has been active as a photography instructor and professor, first at CEGEP du Vieux Montréal from 1971 to 1980, then from 1980 to 1995 at Concordia University where he was appointed Chairman of the Department of Cinema and Photography in 1984. In 1990 he was visiting professor at the Cracow Academy of Fine Arts. He has served as a visiting lecturer at Stanford University in California since 1991.

His work has been widely exhibited and published, both in Canada and abroad. Solo exhibitions include the Canadian Centre for Architecture, Pécs Art Gallery in Hungary, the Cracow Academy of Fine Arts, the Centre George Pompidou in Paris, the Musée d'art contemporain in Montreal, the National Film Board of Canada, the McCord Museum of Canadian History and the Chicago Institute of Design. He has also participated in a number of group exhibitions, and over the years has been active in conferences and workshops.

Principal commissions include the Canadian Centre for Architecture in 1989, 1991 and 1995.

Szilasi's work is represented in the public collections of Air Canada, the Canada Council Art Bank, the Bibiothèque nationale in Montreal, the Canadian Centre for Architecture, the Canadian Museum of Contemporary Photography, the Edmonton Art Gallery, the McCord Museum, Mount Allison University, the Musée d'art contemporain, the Montreal Museum of Fine Arts, the Musée du Québec, the National Gallery in Ottawa, Prêts d'œuvres d'arts, Quebec City and the Stedelijk Museum, Amsterdam, among others.

Szilasi is committed to making people aware of their environment. Both as teacher and as photographer he has influenced a generation with his carefully considered approach to photographing people. He has recorded his subjects within their environments, particularly in rural Quebec regions such as Charlevoix and Beauce counties, Abitibi, Lac Saint-Jean and Lotbinière. His large-format and panoramic photographs of Quebec architecture demonstrate his interest in the built environment.

In 1997 the Montreal Museum of Fine Arts held a retrospective exhibition of Szilasi's photographs, covering the years 1954 to 1996.

Photo collage on board, 1996
14½″ x 20″ (36.8 x 50.8 cm)

GENTILE TONDINO, RCA

ENTILE TONDINO began his art career as a full-time apprentice with Adam Sherriff Scott during the war years. He began formal training in 1948, first at the Montreal School of Art with Alfred Pinsky and Ghitta Caiserman, and then at the Montreal Museum's School of Art and Design, where he specialized in art teaching under Arthur Lismer and Audrey Taylor.

His career of more than forty years has been largely devoted to teaching art. His first posting was at the Montreal Museum's fine-art school. In 1959 he was invited by Professor John Bland to teach part-time at the McGill School of Architecture, where he has been working ever since. He has taught graduate courses since 1975, has served as guest critic, and has taught summer watercolour workshops in the Laurentians and the Eastern Townships. He was elected a member of the Canadian Group of Painters, the outgrowth of the Group of Seven, in 1955. In 1962 he was elected to the Royal Canadian Academy of Art, and in 1968 to the Royal Academy of Art. Since the sixties he has participated on selection committees and juries. He has worked as a restorer and has been commissioned over the years as a portrait painter.

Tondino's exhibition history dates from the 1940s; in the last few years his work has been shown at the annual Eudice Garmaise Exhibition of Contemporary Quebec Professional Artists, annual group exhibitions at Stewart Hall in Pointe-Claire, Quebec, RCA group exhibitions at the Dominion Art Gallery and the Galerie Walter

Klinkoff in Montreal, and Academy House in Toronto. He is represented in the permanent collections of the Montreal Museum of Fine Arts, the National Gallery of Canada, the Firestone Collection, C.I.L., Reader's Digest and Shell Canada as well as in numerous private collections.

"In this painting titled Avmor, *I have worked with a design which is abstract behind the surface image. It is basically made up of vertical and horizontal divisions inherent in the architecture. Each large area made up by these divisions is patterned with arches, columns and rectangles. These elements break down the large shapes to complete the total design of the painting.*

I have not shown the boundary of the property. I let it extend on both sides of the frame, thus giving a feeling that the subject pattern extends further. I feel strongly that the motif which I have created is reflected in other parts of Old Montreal, where there is a repetition in form and decoration which gives unity to the place. In Avmor, *I am contented with the balance I have achieved, the interrelation between the view I have selected, the overall pattern design, the colouring and the mood of the painting."*

Oil on canvas, 1996
54″ x 40″ (101.6 x 78 cm)

RICHARD DINNIS (R.D.) WILSON

RICHARD D. WILSON (1920-1994), a native of Montreal, was educated at the École des Beaux-Arts and attended Royal Canadian Academy classes. His studies were interrupted by the outbreak of World War II, during which he served as a specialist compiling aerial photos into maps that were used by the Allied forces. After the war he returned to Montreal to support his young family through work in design and commercial art and, fascinated by the architecture in Old Montreal, started painting pictures of old buildings in his spare time.

Wilson's experiences in Europe had taught him this appreciation of traditional architecture. In the late 1950s and early 1960s, when the face of Montreal was drastically changing because of demolition and new construction, he made many drawings in the area of the current CBC complex in the east end of the city, and in Old Montreal. This hobby became his livelihood in 1965, soon after the publication of a book in collaboration with Eric McLean called *The Living Past of Montreal*, which featured many of these drawings.

In 1967 he undertook a commission from the Bank of Montreal to mark the bank's 150th anniversary and the nation's centennial. For the Bowater Corporation he produced a series of drawings tracing the stages involved in the creation of paper. He travelled extensively throughout Newfoundland and Labrador, recording its changing face, and in 1971 spent several months abroad touring Israel, Turkey, Spain and Portugal. To commemorate the 300th anniversary of Kingston, Ontario in 1973, he produced a collection of drawings, thirty of which are on display in the City Hall.

A prolific artist, Wilson has been widely collected; more than 200 of his works are housed in the National Archives of Canada.

R. D. Wilson was the first artist commissioned by Av Morrow in 1965. The drawing he produced has been used ever since on the company's seasonal greeting card. Almost thirty years after this first commission, Wilson was once again asked to sketch the Avmor building, but as fate would have it this would be his last creation. He finished the drawing on December 7th, 1994 and was tragically killed by a bus the very next day while crossing Côte Saint-Luc Road with his portfolio in hand. This gentle and humble artist is sadly missed by his friends at Avmor.

Pen and ink on paper, 1994
17½" x 22" (44.4 x 55.9 cm)

Pen and ink on paper, 1965
25" x 20" (63.5 x 50.8 cm)

SERGE CHAPLEAU

Born in Montreal in 1945, Serge Chapleau displayed an early aptitude for drawing. In 1969 he graduated from the École des Beaux-Arts and three years later was the first person in Canada to publish a full-colour, full-page cartoon. He went on to contribute as political cartoonist to the Sunday edition of *Montréal-Matin* and, among others, *Week-End*, *Actualité*, and *Nous*. During this period he created a series of three-dimensional puppets for television, including the famous and still active Gérard D. Laflaque.

In 1985 Chapleau joined *Le Devoir* and, apart from a term with *Matin* and *7 jours*, he remained there until 1996, when he moved to *La Presse*. Chapleau defines a political cartoonist as someone who is "extremely lucky, because he can stick his tongue out in public and get paid for it."

Pencil on paper, 1998
11⅜" x 11⅜" (29 x 29 cm)

VIEUX MONTRÉAL-Two women dig out their car after the ice storm of January, 1998

Ink on paper, 1998
13″ x 8⅛″ (33 x 20.6 cm)

TERRY MOSHER (Aislin)

Aislin is the name of Terry Mosher's elder daughter and the pen name he uses as the political cartoonist for the *Montreal Gazette*. Syndicated throughout Canada, his work has appeared in the *New York Times*, *Time*, the *National Lampoon*, *Harper's*, the *Atlantic Monthly*, and *Punch*.

Mosher was born in Ottawa 54 years ago. He attended fourteen different schools in Montreal, Toronto, and Quebec City, graduating from Montreal's École des Beaux-Arts in 1967. He has travelled extensively, writing and drawing interpretive sketchbooks throughout Canada, the United States, Northern Ireland, Russia, Cuba, and North Africa.

The recipient of two National Newspaper Awards and five individual prizes from the International Salon of Caricature, Mosher was inducted into the Canadian News Hall of Fame in 1985.

JONAS ASPLER, JEREMY DUCHARME

Jonas Aspler (aged 17) and Jeremy Ducharme (aged 19) learned photography as part of the Leave Out ViolencE (L.O.V.E.) photojournalism project. L.O.V.E. is a multi-cultural, community-based outreach organization that uses creative programming to help sensitize youth about violence. L.O.V.E. provides a community of support to balance one of the major causes of youth violence: the fragmentation of society.

In the photojournalism project, teenagers learn to analyse the causes, impact and prevention of violence. They are then trained to take their photographs and writing into public schools, community centres and public exhibitions, where they lead workshops on the issue of violence prevention.

"We chose this picture because it gave a different perspective of the Avmor building, especially because of the contrasts. As a first professional job, this picture was challenging for us."

Photograph, 1996
11″ x 14″ (27.9 x 35.6 cm)

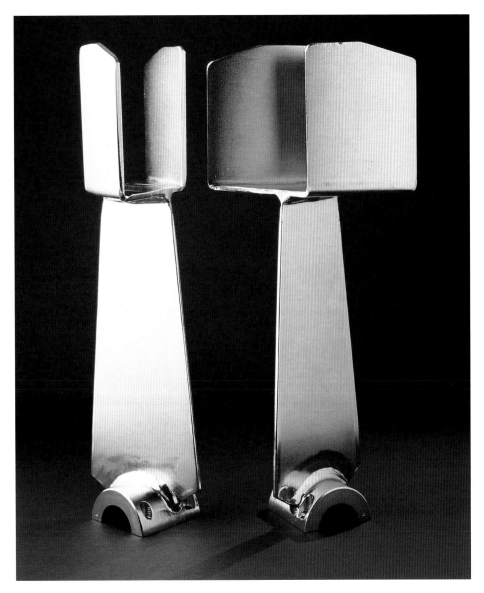

KINETIC SCULPTURE

Fascinated by the unusual blades used in man-ufacturing Avmor's liquid emultion polymers, Av Morrow conceived of this intriguing kinetic sculpture. His vision was made concrete by the Engineering Group at Avmor and a contest was held within the company to find a name for it. Of the many suggestions put forward, the clear winner was the title "Réflection/Reflexions."

As the polished stainless steel blades rotate, they appear almost to touch each other and their reflection in the mirrored background enhances the kinetic effect.

Réflexions / Reflexions
Polished stainless steel, 1997
21″ x 9¾ x 4″ (53.5 x 24.5 x 10.2 cm)

JULI (LULU) MORROW

Lulu's earliest memories of painting are of her Auntie Leah's kitchen in an apartment on Linton Avenue in Montreal, where she created a mural on a roll of white shelf paper taped on to the wall. Today, her painting locations include Martha's Vineyard, Mustique and (mostly) a little room with a big window off her bedroom in Toronto.

When not dabbling with paints (she has had no formal training in painting or perspective) and creating a name as a very amateur artist among her friends, Juli is mostly known as the daughter of Av and Dora Morrow, and the mother of Rebecca and Molly Brennan.

Juli fills her remaining time practising law as a partner in the Toronto law firm of Goodman Philips & Vineberg, having attained B.C.L. and LL.B degrees from McGill University and a LL. M from the University of Toronto.

Her work hangs in her office, along with that of several professional artists.

Juli lives in Toronto with her husband, Arthur Brennan, and her two daughters.

Acrylic on canvas, 1997
22″ x 27″ (55.8 x 68.6 cm)

REBECCA MORROW BRENNAN

WHILE Rebecca has concentrated her artistic efforts during the past year in her pottery classes, with colourful and useful results, she also enjoys other forms of expression including, most recently, painting with acrylics.

Rebecca has just completed Grade 5 at Bialik Hebrew Day School in Toronto, as well as Grade 2 Piano at the Royal Conservatory of Music. She lives in Toronto with her mother (Juli Morrow), father (Arthur Brennan) and little sister (Molly), and loves visits from her grandparents (Dora and Av Morrow).

Rebecca enjoys reading, swimming, playing tennis, riding her bike, and drama.

This past year she got rave reviews in her role as Tetina in the school play.

Rebecca also likes to spend time with her friends, who often get together and create magic with various media, including beads, "model magic," "pop-ups" and chalk.

Acrylic on canvas, 1997, 12″ x 16″ (30.5 x 40.7 cm)

MOLLY MORROW BRENNAN

MOLLY MORROW BRENNAN is a creative young artist who has just completed a very successful year in Grade 2 at Bialik Hebrew Day School in Toronto, where she produced several well-received three dimensional works using boxes, paint, paper and string.

Molly has recently devoted much of her artistic time to creating masterpieces in coloured chalk on the driveway of her home in Toronto but she intends to revert to a more lasting medium when she visits her grandparents' Dora and Av Morrow's home on Martha's Vineyard with its bright painting studio.

Molly lives with her mother (Juli Morrow), father (Arthur Brennan) and big sister (Rebecca) and no pets yet. She enjoys discovering and learning about nature.

Acrylic on canvas, 1997, 12″ x 16″ (30.5 x 40.7 cm)

AVRUM MORROW

Acrylic on canvas, 1997
20″ x 24″ (50.8 x 61 cm)

THE STORY OF AVMOR

AVMOR was founded in 1948 by Avrum Morrow and Henry Chinks. Av Morrow had studied engineering and physics at McGill University; Henry Chinks, his brother-in-law, was a well-known commercial building manager. Both were eager to break with family tradition – the garment-manufacturing business – and start a fresh business of their own. They began their operation with a unique product called "Odorite", a door-controlled deodorizer to be installed in public washrooms.

Among the pictures in the Avmor Collection, one stands out as being not about Sainte-Hélène Street but about the early days of the Avmor company. It is a collage, done in 1966 by Normand Hudon, and among its elements is a cheque issued to Avmor in 1948 by Ruby Foo's Restaurant. It is for $4.50, which represents the cost of renting three Odorite units for one month. Another cheque is for $18.00 from Henry Morgan's, the department store, for the use of twelve units in its washrooms. Other elements in Hudon's collage include Avmor's first kettles, in which it made its products, and its first storage tanks. And there are also fragments of snapshots of the company's first employees.

Soon after its success with Odorite, Avmor added various other products to its catalogue of items to service buildings, such as waxes, soaps, deodorants and disinfectants. To meet the growing demand, the company established its own laboratory and manufacturing facilities, and opened service routes to Ottawa and the Eastern Townships.

Avmor accomplished a major breakthrough in 1973 with the development of liquid emulsion-polymers, basic to the manufacture of floor finishes and sanders. In 1980 the company launched the first made-in-Canada electrical hand dryer for public washrooms, and soon NOVA became the leading national brand. It is now sold in nearly thirty countries, including England, France, the U.S. and Poland. NOVA hand dryers can be found in the Tokyo Railway Station and the Taj Mahal Hotel in India. Other Avmor products are sold in some forty countries, including the U.S., France, Great Britain, China, India, Japan and Hong Kong.

Today, Avmor has a fully equipped research and quality-control laboratory, winning awards for its commitment to creating environmentally useful products. But in 1948 the company opened its first office in what Av Morrow describes as a "closet in a small clothing factory". In 1953 Avmor moved to its Sainte-Hélène Street home.

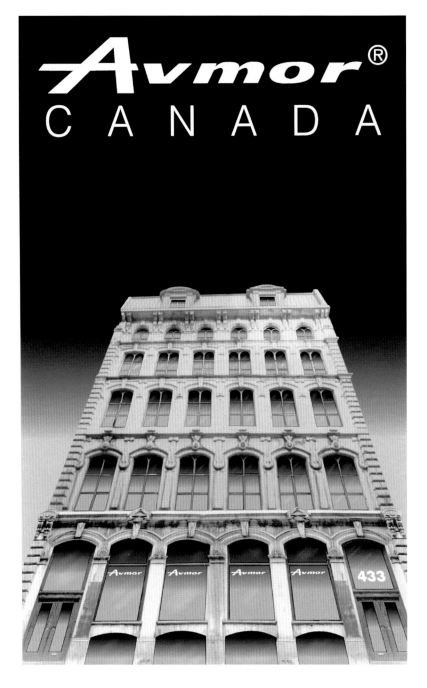

Advertising poster created from a digitized photo of the Avmor building, by Luc Ladouceur, 1993.

A BRIEF HISTORY

Avmor Ltd. was established in 1948, and incorporated with a Canadian federal charter on April 17, 1950. We are now fifty years old and continue to be young.

NOTEWORTHY DATES:

1948 – first address at 394 Dorchester Street West, before it was widened in 1952. The street is now known as René-Lévesque Boulevard

1948 – first product was Odorite, a door-controlled deodorizer for public washrooms

1953 – moved to 431 Sainte-Hélène Street (25,000 sq. ft.)

1955 – began producing and marketing soaps and waxes

1963 – expanded to 433 Sainte-Hélène Street (30,000 sq. ft.)

1963 – began manufacturing detergents and disinfectants

1964 – set up Canada wide Avmor Distrubutors

1972 – acquired the parking lot at the corner of Sainte-Hélène Street and LeMoyne Street (10,000 sq. ft.)

1972 – developed unique liquid-emulsion polymer technology trademarked Hetrogenic Quadra Polymer

1974 – expanded to 445 Sainte-Hélène Street (30,000 sq. ft., for a total space of 85,000 sq. ft.)

1980 – developed the Biomaxx bag-in-box soap system

1981 – developed the Nova electric hand-dryer now sold in over 35 countries

1988 – purchased Cleancare International, a manufacturer of industrial and institutional carpet cleaning equipment

1989 – developed various plastic items for sanitation and cleaning industry (i.e. safety signs, toilet-bowl mops, deodorant cabinets, urinal screens)

1990 – acquired Fuller Brush Co. (Canada), a national brand manufacturer of cleaning chemicals and sanitation hardware

1991 – leased 57,000 sq. ft. distribution centre and electro mechanical manufacturing facility

1992 – developed Export Division, which now sells cleaning chemicals worldwide

1992 – developed new improved polymer technology now licenced in other parts of the world, trademarked Pentapolymer

1993 – created Avmor Retail Division to service the retail industry throughout Canada

1994 – introduced three-language, four-colour product catalogue (English, French and Spanish)

1996 – inaugurated a new R & D laboratory with a mission to develop new and better polymers and cleaning products

1996 – Avmor went on the Internet and offered E.D.I. (Electronic Data Interface)

Avmor Mission Statement

Our mission is to be the leader in the manufacture of cleaning, sanitation and maintenance products that are ecologically correct and environmentally friendly, and to introduce and successfully market the Avmor brand around the world. We are also committed to the continual improvement of our Nova hand dryer and to making it widely accepted as the hand-drying method of choice — both in the workplace and in public washrooms worldwide.

We will strive for these goals for the benefit of all our customers, employees and suppliers. We want every Avmor employee to develop his or her full potential and be recognized as a valued participant in Avmor's success.

Enoncé de mission d'Avmor

Nous avons pour mission d'être le chef de file dans le domaine de la fabrication de produits de nettoyage, d'hygiène et d'entretien qui sont écologiques et sans danger pour l'environnement, et de faire connaître les produits Avmor et d'en assurer avec succès la commercialisation à l'échelle internationale. Nous nous engageons également à assurer l'amélioration constante de notre séchoir Nova pour les mains pour en faire un appareil de premier choix tant sur les lieux de travail que dans les toilettes publiques du monde entier.

Nous nous efforcerons d'atteindre ces objectifs pour le bénéfice de tous nos clients, employés et fournisseurs. Nous voulons que chaque employé d'Avmor réalise son plein potentiel et qu'il soit reconnu pour son rôle essentiel au succès d'Avmor.

COLLECTION INDEX

52 – 53
OSBORNE, Sean
Collage on board, 1993
4 panels, each 31″ x 38½″ (78.7 x 97.7 cm)

55
PANTEL, Gerri
Acrylic on cotton, 1996
14″ x 18″ (35.6 x 45.7 cm)

57
PIVET, Pierre
Oil on canvas, 1995
36″ x 30″ (91.4 x 76.2 cm)

59
SEGAL, Seymour
Oil on canvas, 1996
33½″ x 39½″ (85 x 100.3 cm)

61
SZILASI, Gabor
Photo collage on board, 1996
14½″ x 20″ (36.8 x 50.8 cm)

63
TONDINO, Gentile
Oil on canvas, 1996
54″ x 40″ (101.6 x 78 cm)

64
WILSON, R.D.
Pen and ink on paper, 1994
17½″ x 22″ (44.4 x 55.9 cm)

65
WILSON, R.D.
Pen and ink on paper, 1965
25″ x 20″ (63.5 x 50.8 cm)

66
CHAPLEAU, Serge
Pencil on paper, 1998
11⅜″ x 11⅜″ (29 x 29 cm)

67
MOSHER, Terry
Ink on paper, 1998
13″ x 8⅛″ (33 x 20.6 cm)

68
ASPLER, Jonas/DUCHARME, Jeremy
Photograph, 1996
11″ x 14″ (27.9 x 35.6 cm)

69
KINETIC SCULPTURE
Polished stainless steel, 1997
21″ x 9¾ x 4″ (53.5 x 24.5 x 10.2 cm)

70
MORROW, Juli
Oil on canvas, 1997
22″ x 27″ (55.8 x 68.6 cm)

71
BRENNAN MORROW, Rebecca
Acrylic on canvas, 1997
12″ x 16″ (30.5 x 40.7 cm)

71
BRENNAN MORROW, Molly
Acrylic on canvas, 1997
12″ x 16″ (30.5 x 40.7 cm)

72
MORROW, Avrum
Acrylic on canvas, 1997
20″ x 24″ (50.8 x 61 cm)

A copy of the AVMOR COLLECTION
has been deposited in the libraries
of the following institutions.

❧❧

Une copie de cet ouvrage a été déposée
à la bibliothèque
des institutions suivantes.

— CANADA —

Carleton University, School of Architecture

Canadian Centre for Architecture

Concordia University

Dalhousie University

L'Université du Québec à Montréal,
Département de Design

McGill University, School of Architecture

Technical University of Nova Scotia,
Faculty of Architecture

Université Laval,
Faculté d'architecture et d'aménagement

University of British Columbia,
School of Architecture

University of Calgary, Faculty of Environmental
Design Architecture Program

University of Manitoba,
Department of Landscape Architecture

University of Toronto,
Department of Landscape Architecture

University of Waterloo, School of Architecture

Université de Montréal, Faculté de l'aménagement

Université de Montréal, École d'architecture

— U.S.A. —

Art Director Club, New York, New York.

Brown University, Department of History of Art
and Architecture

Carnegie Mellon University,
Department of Architecture

Century Association, New York, New York.

Chilmark Public Library, Chilmark, Massachusetts

Columbia University, Graduate School
of Architecture, Planning and Preservation

Cornell University, Department of Architecture

Frank Lloyd Wright School of Architecture

Harvard University, Graduate School of Design

Kent State University, School of Architecture
and Environment Design

MIT School of Architecture and Planning

Pennsylvania State University,
Department of Architectural Engineering

Princeton University, School of Architecture

Purdue University, Department of
Landscape Architecture

Smithsonian Institute, Washington, D.C.

The Municipal Art Society, New York, New York.

University of California, Berkeley,
Department of Architecture

Yale University, School of Architecture

— UNITED KINGDOM —

Oxford Brookes University, School of Architecture

University of Cambridge, Department of Architecture

— EUROPE —

Technical University of Vienna,
Architecture and Urban Planning

Oulu University, Department of Architecture

École d'Architecture de Normandie

Istituto Universitario di Architettura di Venezia

Rotterdam Academy of Architecture

Oslo, School of Architecture

Royal Institute of Technology, Department of
Architecture and Town Planning, Sweden

— AUSTRALIA —

University of Melbourne,
Faculty of Architecture, Building and Planning

University of Sydney, Faculty of Architecture

— ASIA —

University of Hong Kong, Faculty of Architecture